Dear Reader,

The book you are holding came about in a rather different way to most others. It was funded directly by readers through a new website: Unbound. Unbound is the creation of three writers. We started the company because we believed there had to be a better deal for both writers and readers. On the Unbound website, authors share the ideas for the books they want to write directly with readers. If enough of you support the book by pledging for it in advance, we produce a beautifully bound special subscribers' edition and distribute a regular edition and e-book wherever books are sold, in shops and online.

This new way of publishing is actually a very old idea (Samuel Johnson funded his dictionary this way). We're just using the internet to build each writer a network of patrons. At the back of this book, you'll find the names of all the people who made it happen.

Publishing in this way means readers are no longer just passive consumers of the books they buy, and authors are free to write the books they really want. They get a much fairer return too – half the profits their books generate, rather than a tiny percentage of the cover price.

If you're not yet a subscriber, we hope that you'll want to join our publishing revolution and have your name listed in one of our books in the future. To get you started, here is a £5 discount on your first pledge. Just visit unbound.com, make your pledge and type **SHEPHERD5** in the promo code box when you check out.

Thank you for your support,

Dan, Justin and John
Founders, Unbound

THE SHEPHERD'S HUT

The Genius of Shakespeare

The Cure for Love

The Song of the Earth

John Clare: A Biography

Soul of the Age

English Literature: A Very Short Introduction

Being Shakespeare: A One-Man Play for Simon Callow

Ted Hughes: The Unauthorised Life

The Shepherd's Hut

POEMS

Jonathan Bate

with illustrations by Emma Bridgewater

Unbound

This edition first published in 2017

Unbound

6th Floor Mutual House, 70 Conduit Street, London W1S 2GF

www.unbound.com

Illustrations © Emma Bridgewater

Text design by Patty Rennie

A CIP record for this book is available from the British Library

ISBN 978-1-78352-429-7 (trade hbk)
ISBN 978-1-78352-430-3 (ebook)
ISBN 978-1-78352-431-0 (limited edition)

Printed in Great Britain by Clays Ltd, St Ives Plc

1 3 5 7 9 8 6 4 2

MIX
Paper from
responsible sources
FSC® C018179

For Ian Huish

CONTENTS

ELEGIES

HOMAGES

CARPE DIEM

Slow Reading

Take time for each word,
Give room to white space,
Listen for the beat,
Tune to the weather,
Rekindle memory,
Life-scape and heart-leap.

Know that poetry
is not of the world:
It is in the worth
of the words to you,
Patient reader, open
to the spirit of slow.

All royalties from this book will be donated to the work of ReLit,
a foundation devoted to slow reading as a form of stress relief.

PASTORALS

The Swans on Our Lake

The diet of swans is mainly vegetarian:
pondweed, stonewort and widgeon grass,
sea arrow, salt marsh and eelgrass,
club-rush, milfoil and green algae.
But they occasionally indulge
in tadpole and mollusc.

Sometimes you see one fold its leg upon its back
to adjust body temperature,
rather as an elephant's ear
absorbs the heat of the sun.
They sleep standing on one leg
or afloat with head tucked under wing.

The ungentlemanly behaviour depicted in the story of Leda
is uncharacteristic:
they mate for life and know the meaning of grief.
Some bereaved swans stay alone for the rest of their lives
while others take flight and rejoin their flock.

The other myth is true:
when they lie dying
they breathe their only song,
a long, low honk as air vacates their lungs.

They are said to be loyal servants of the queen.

The Man Who Had Not Written a Poem for Years

As the sand trickled through his fingers
The boy looked at the sea.
Spume flecks near, tanker hulks far.
The race was on.
All the sails working with the wind:
White, striped and zig-zag.
His heart racing, he ran along the sand.

As the sand trickled through the glass
The man looked at the lake.
Weir rustle near, bending tree far.
The words were flowing.
All his mind was working with the muse:
Poem, prose and letter.
His heart leaping, he was the boy again.

The Quad from Our Window

Forward and back
following string and peg
he mows the ancient quad
in concentric circles or
in waves like icons of signal strength

and across the steep banks they go

once it must have been with scythes
but now a Flymo is held on ropes
the team pulling together

perfection of the lines
clipped finish of the edge
all in an order echoing

to the symmetry of cloister
fanlight, keystone
architrave and tracery

an honouring of the old ways.

Banjaran

(FOR H. R. H.)

Paleozoic limestone
Geothermal hot springs

Cascades from the rainforest
You climb to the cave
holding the bamboo rail
and the heavy air is scented

When you look down
the steam rises from the pools
and it is your cares and duties that

evaporate

Tang Variations

Twelve improvisations on ancient Chinese poems by
Wang Wei, Pei Di, Zu Young, Meng Haoran, Li Bai, Wang Zhihuan

1. *Deer Enclosure*
Empty mountain. Seeing nobody.
Only hearing the sound of voices.
Reflection: sunlight enters the deep forest
And shines again on green moss.

2. *House in the Bamboo Grove*
Sitting alone deep in a remote thicket
I pluck my lute and sing.
In this dark, unknown forest
The bright moon shines on me.

3. *Goodbye*
We go to the mountain for our farewell.
At sunset I close the door in the brushwood fence;
Next year the spring grass will be green
And you, prince among friends, will return or not return.

4. *One Heart*
Red beans grow in the south country.
In the warm weather there will be many branches.
I want you to be here to pluck them with me.
That is the thing I yearn for: it will cure my heart.

5. *Arrival*

You come from our old village
With news of home.
Tomorrow by the silk-lined window edge
Tell me if the late-winter plum is yet in flower.

6. *A Farewell*

If you return to the mountains and the valleys
You must find beauty in the heights and the depths:
Don't follow the example of the man
Who never travels beyond the peach garden where we play.

7. *Snowy Peak*

The north peak of Zhongnan is beautiful:
The snow piled up to the floating clouds.
The sky is a blue clearing above the treetops
And the city below chills with the sunset.

8. *Mooring at Night on Jiande River*

Steering his boat to its berth beside the mist-smoke river
The failing light brings new sadness to the traveller,
A wilderness of sky dwarfing the trees
But the clear river brings him close to the moon.

9. *Spring Morning*

Spring sleep does not feel the dawn
It hears the birds singing everywhere.
The night came with the sound of wind and rain
And I wonder how many blossoms fell.

10. *Quiet Night Thinking*
Bright moonlight on my bed
Like frost on hardened ground.
I raise my head and look at that bright moon;
I bow my head and think of my old home.

11. *Love's Bitterness*
A beautiful woman rolls a pearled blind;
In deep stillness she sits with a slight frown,
Eyebrow like a moth, tears traced on her cheeks,
She cries with regret or hatred in her heart.

12. *Climbing White Stork Tower*
The white sun sets behind the mountain,
The Yellow River flows into the sea;
If you want to see a thousand miles
Then go up another floor, always up.

Arboreal Cousin

They bussed us bumpily from Sandakan
Told us to wait below a certain tree

High in the air a rope stretched its long span
Suspended below the green canopy

You slap a mosquito – you wait in hope –
It begins to vibrate – you catch your breath –

He comes hand across hand along the rope
Unhurried towards the inviting leaf

Pongo pygmaeus – better in Malay –
Orang, person, *hutan*, of the forest

You've been waiting all your life for today
Your boyhood dream to be a conservationist

His genome has been sequenced in the lab
He is ninety-seven per cent pure man

He climbs the platform where there's fruit to grab
Hangs by an arm, then leg, then leg and arm

Then he performs a slowmo pirouette
Executed purely for his own delight

The rope twitches again, our eyes follow
The young one striding on, almost flying

We doubletake to see her bald from top to toe –
When they rescued her she was infected, dying

The antibiotic was made for us
It took every thread of her orange coat

And with the fur it stripped the three per cent
So in her nakedness she is all of us

Sepilok, North Borneo

11

Kydonia

Strabo said it was the city of King Minos
Others named it for his grandson Kydon,
Born of Akakallis and Hermes the god
(Or was it maybe Apollo?),
Left in the wild and suckled by a dog.

Their totem was the bull, emerging from the waves
So beautiful that they refused
To cast its mass and life
Back to Poseidon's realm.
He raged. The bull raged.
Pasiphae fell for it.

Now the carved bulls are stacked high
In the museum by the harbour.
'Unpublished. No photographs.'
The archaeologist who made the find
Cannot bear to let his story go.

They sell wooden bull pizzles on the tourist stands
And all that now emerges from the waves
Is the endangered sea-turtle
Graceful in its domed shell,
Waving an insouciant flipper.

Aegean

You saw a red-footed falcon ride
A thermal high over the bay of Zeus,
Motionless and watching before he swoops
His plummet through azure to aquamarine.
There is beauty and terror in the fall,
The second when a world is split asunder
And a shadow cast across the sea.
But greater beauty, deeper joy, as he
Soars back to air and sun, his stomach-churn
Moment of mad descent etched in memory
As marker buoy of rock and quicksand.
So all I ask is that you turn your eye
From that perilous descent and follow
His flight as he rebounds and beckons you on.

Andelle Valley

I walk between the village and the beech wood.
Across the fields the old square church
echoes its bell-call to the back-bent man
(motionless in contemplation of his garden
he becomes the land itself)
but only the crow responds and the duck takes flight.

The forest is always the other side of the river.
Up there, under gold and brown, a farmer claimed
he shot a wolf.

A fish plops down as the river disappears
and the dog is no longer at my heels.
By the time I return
the kingfishers have gone.

The horses either side of the river
call to each other and canter away,
a musk rat dives and vanishes as
the river itself comes to a
dead end
of backwater.

Easter Snow on Dartmoor

Where the moor lies frozen still
Muffled steps mark out the way,
Climb towards the covered hill
Fading light of April day.

Flakes that drift and almost speak,
Flakes that cover tree and ground
Touch a face and chill a cheek
Feathers drop without a sound.

And then the snow caught fire
Below the falling sky,
With all-consuming power
A hand stretched out on high
And pulled me in its wake
Stretching soul to brink of break.

Retreat

(i)
A sparrow-song in country chapel eaves
Damp-dry faces: mist and wind at playful wrestling
Communion sip of spirit in the mouth
The smell of fresh-mown grass among the leaves
Horizon-sharpness of the sun in spring –

Five windows for the soul to look on truth.

(ii)
Where oozing Ouse has burst its banks
and water laps the graveyard wall,
two walkers pass a morning word –

'The gulls have found an inland sea...'
'Look! Brent geese swimming in the field...'
'Those eight nests in the rookery...'

Telegraph poles rise from the deep;
trees creak like doors in ghost stories,
their roots undermined.
                              Old houses:
thatch drops, black beams bend, white walls bulge.

The bridleway to Houghton church
cannot be passed:
the waters of the flood have not
subsided yet.

*Written at the Community of the Resurrection's
retreat house in Hemingford Grey, Cambridgeshire*

Broadstairs

(WITH APOLOGIES TO MATTHEW ARNOLD)

When I was a child
this resort was always summer:
crowded beach, suntan lotion air,
high-tide cricket in the Victoria Gardens
or coloured evening fairy-lights.

I have been here since to walk the sea-line,
wandered over rock-weeds in yellow autumn light
collecting driftwood for the scone-hearth fire,
a lone
gull on turning waves.

Or at Easter
seen the moon on a clear night
above tingle sea and lightship beam
that sweeps the mill-pond surface
in thirty-second pinpoint glow
to catch a passing present
and strike my eyes.

But this last return is August winter:
no six o'clock bucket and spade trek
to boarding-house dinner
and washing sandy toes.
Just empty beach, broken deckchair,
stale cornet blown on esplanade
burnt-out bandstand, rusted children's train
and shuttered hut of one-leg beach photographer.

Mist off the straits,
Bleak House shrouded
and foghorn sounding.

The sea has disappeared
and I am confused by night that should be day.

Spirit of Place

Afterwards I realised it was like a Forster novel:
at the time we were too busy hurrying for the bus,
hiding behind heavy Tuscan ladies to skip the fare.

At Fiesole we failed to make our rendezvous,
hung around the sleepy square, then took our chance
to pose for cameras in the Roman theatre –

The view was best away and to the north,
an illicit peep behind the scenes when attention
should have been fixed on the sunset stage.

Oh yes, sunset over Florence, storm-clouds in the air,
a dream beyond all expectation –
so that's how masters painted here.

We wandered up a lane 'unchanged since Dante's day',
the city sprawled in haze below, a gardener at his vines
scraped the fine dry soil (and yet his grapes still grow).

The rain sent us scurrying for the postcard stall:
we browsed as if about to buy a souvenir
for twenty minutes till the bus returned.

Down it wound us, swinging on the strap,
and the short sharp shower had ended
when we reached the Duomo and clambered out.

Although the pavement was wet and smelt of dust,
we still could sit on the steps of San Lorenzo
eating pizzas. Giotto would have loved it.

The Shepherd's Hut

is olive-green outside,
on wheels
by our lake, camouflaged
like a twitcher's hide
for watching heron, swan
and morning flash
of kingfisher blue.

Within, it's cream
which makes you think
of old-time milkmaids
and lambs-wool insulation
and then of Gabriel Oak

(his was cosy and alluring,
the scarlet handful of fire
in addition to the candle reflecting
its own genial colour
upon whatever it could reach;
in ours there are books and mineral water
in place of turpentine, tar, magnesia, ginger
and castor-oil)

It smells of woodsmoke, cedar and cherry blossom
and when the rain hits the corrugated iron
of the cold tin roof
it sounds like Scarlatti's cat
or the drumming of life, life, life.

Although it's meant as solitude's haven
into which the muse descends,
it was only fully christened
when we pulled the sofa into a bed
and lay all night
with the top half
of the stable door open
to reveal the flickering light
on low-hanging branches
of the candles under storm-glasses
lighting the path
from circumstance and pomp
to simpler, bigger things.

AMORS

Beginning

Fingertips at play in the smoke-filled air
Still the face beneath its mask
Eyes that cannot see for fear

Shadow of a candle dancing on the wall
Words that cut the crafted silence
The embryo fights within its shell

Open-handed she cups the chick
And holds the beating of a heart
Breathe gently and the wave will break.

Laforgue's Image

In short,
I was going to give myself with an
'I love you.'
But then I realised
(not without a stab of pain inside)
that in the first place
I didn't even possess myself.

Three Kisses from the Greek Anthology

As we said goodnight under sunset skies,
Our lips joined in the rapture of a kiss.
I know the things we said were never lies,
But did I only dream the tongue-tied bliss?
If I was transported to paradise,
How is it that I'm back on earth and lost?

Her kiss is no more than the graze of lips;
With lightest touch she works upon your mouth.
The thing to worry about is her breath:
It'll drain your soul from heart to fingertips.

Dear Melissa: you're named after the bee.
Aptly, because there's nectar on your tongue,
Honey to taste when our lips join as one –
And you sting me when you demand your fee.

Titania and the Neuroscientist

Love's chemistry sings
Crazy for you
Mad about the boy...

Shakespeare calls it love-in-idleness:
The purple flower *Viola tricolor*
Colloquially known as
Wild pansy, heartsease, Johnny jump up,
Jack come up and kiss me, three faces in a hood,
Tickle my fancy, come and cuddle me,
Or heart's delight.
Crushed by a fairy and placed on your eyelid
It'll make you fall in love with the next person you see
Be he Adonis or an ass.

Neurophysiologists call it an effect of monoamines and hormones.
The dopamine rush (same as a cocaine high),
The norepinephrine that really gets you going
And makes you notice every tiny detail
(The way he moves his hand, the dimple of her smile).
Then there's the serotonin that drives you to the edge,
The oxytocin orgasm that binds you close
As mother and baby on breast.
And above all the PEA.
Ah yes, phenylethylamine: it makes you giddy
And kills your appetite for anything but love.

The lunatic, the lover, the poet
And the neuroscientist
Are of imagination all compact.
They know that cheeks flush, palms sweat,
Heart races and you walk on air,
You cannot sleep, you cannot eat,
Your mind can think of nothing else.

Echo fell in love with Narcissus
But he only loved himself,
So she pined away and died.
Only her voice remained,
The trace of love.

The unreciprocated phenylethylamine release
Led to fatal self-starvation.

I think I prefer the Shakespearean version of the old, old story.

Found in France

Paris
Lodestone of poets and lovers, this is our city:
We allow ourselves the cliché because it's true.
We follow in their footsteps along the Left Bank.
We sing to their ghosts and possess their words.
The river flows under each bridge on which
We have told our love as the current calls
With the memory that every sorrow
We have shared has been pursued by joy.
We stand face to face, hand in hand, our arms a bridge
As we long for the night.

Le train bleu
After the oysters and champagne
In the gilded and mirrored restaurant,
After the coupled carriage of the night,
We pull up the blind of the berth
And peel away the carapace of grey,
Recharged with the light of the south.

Villefranche
It was something to do with the presence of the past:
The old Riviera, the Grand Hotel on the Cap,
The cocktail waiter and the cocky *plagiste*,
The blend of Fitzgerald and Bardot,
The brightness in her eyes
When she waved from the boat
And the spring in her step
As she disembarked into her future.

Photograph

I know there's mischief in that smile,
But I see more of kindness and of charm.
The camera flash is bouncing back
From the razor-edge of her high-boned cheek
To leave two dazzling pools of pearl
That dance beside the earring jewel
And play above the white of teeth
(Which will bite if ever she is crossed –
But cross her who would dare and why?)

Her hair is threaded brown and gold
Her eyes are the blue of her dress
Her hand on hip is full assured
Her rings are glinting in the sun
Her face is a mask in shape of a heart,
A heart that's aching for a lover lost
In a chasm below the curve of her breast.

The Rose Cure

I never promised you a rose garden.
This one was thrust upon you unawares,
Accessorised with wingfoot Mercury
And salvaged heads of two startled Caesars.
These are old English roses, musky pink,
Blooming once in May before they shoot away.
Alone you sat there all through that summer,
Below wisteria on surrounding walls,
Scenting the underplanted lavender,
Immoveable in a hatched wicker chair,
Tracing memories around the boxed parterre,
Lacrimae rerum or thoughts too deep for tears.
When autumn came the chair was packed away,
The last petal dropped, and your heart was healed.

After Victor Hugo

Tomorrow at dawn, at the moment of whitefall,
I will go. You see, I know you're waiting for me.
I'll go through the forest and over the mountain.
I cannot live apart from you any longer.

I will walk, eyes fixed and thoughtful,
Walk deaf and blind to all around,
Alone, unknown, back bent, hands clasped.
And the day for me shall be night.

I shall not gaze at the gold of nightfall,
The distant sails unfurling over Harfleur;
And when I arrive I will take a bunch
Of green holly and flowering heather,

And lay it on your grave.

Ending

Love surrendered in evening light,
sent us walking on fallen rose petals:
I would have liked to glue them on again –
perhaps I wanted to believe in gods,
summon Phaeton to whirl our time backwards.
But you showed me that sunshine has to die,
you knew that if we tried to plant them now
next year's roses would be stillborn.
Sun-cool and leaf-fall: in autumn bareness
I stand where you have made me see myself;
I cannot hate you, I am not angry –
only sad that we will never touch hands
on crisp frost under golden light.
                          Only in poems
will you run and catch the featherfall leaves,
stand kissing raindrops from each other's face.
And I have nothing to say
but thank you for that summer.

ELEGIES

For a Funeral

What shame or limit can there be in our regret
And love for one so dear? Teach me the saddest song,
O Tragic Muse, blessed by *your* father with the gift
    Of voice so sweet in lyric song.
So does Quintilius now sleep the longest sleep?
To match him in modesty, twin virtue justice,
Perfect unchanging faith or dedicated truth,
    Will we ever find an equal?
Though lamented by no small number of good men,
None wept more truly for him than you, my Virgil;
Yet, devout as you are, you cannot ask the gods
    To lend him to us once again:
Were you more alluring than Thracian Orpheus,
Able to strike the lyre, seduce the listening trees,
You still could not revive the pale bloodless shade
    Now guided onward by the rod
Of Mercury, who will not relax fate's decree
But lead us all into the darkness and silence.
It is hard: but the pain of what we cannot change
    Is relieved by patient waiting.

After Horace, Odes, *I. xxiv*

41

Omphalos

(IN MEMORY OF R. M. B.)

'Orbilius among the Greeks':
a comedy we couldn't write.
He was dead by then,
would never see the wind
breezing once in Euphrosyne's hair.

Above the olive groves
sun-burnt dust choked the stadium floor.
No one can dream the chariots
back to life.

He never came here.
By chance the war broke out
and plans were changed.

Beyond the olive groves
a bank of empty seats,
dry weeds in the orchēstra.
All the tragedies have been played out.

He never drank here,
not even now Castalia
is a tourists' trickle.

Among the olive groves
we sat and watched black specks:
goats over on Parnassus side,
their bells must echo for miles around.

The atoms of Lucretius?
your spirit might be gathered here.

Letter to Diana

You were the sister I never had.
My cousin, you stayed with us each week in term,
Brought hardback stories from your home –
The Horse and his Boy, *The Silver Chair* –
In my bunk bed I devoured them nightly,
Unable to contain excitement for the next.

And I remember
Seaside summers
Garden teas
Dogs and tortoises.

You married a hippie. That did not end well.
Then you moved to a half-built house
Banked on a hillside across from Hergest Ridge.
Your second love had convinced himself
That the world was on the brink of ending:
You made those hills your nuclear-free zone.
Glastonbury and Greenham were your compass points.
The house was never finished, clutter-strewn,
Always full of children, love and laughter.

When you moved down into the border town
You became a fixture of the community,
Riding your old tricycle through the streets,
Giving new life to the drop-in centre,
Teaching maths to the kids from the estate.

You smiled through every adversity,
Lived by a creed of kindness.

You were the first in my generation to die.
The cancer made you angry.
But then you found your peace in the natural
Burial ground below that hillside house.

They wheeled you out in a basket coffin
On a carriage like a pram,
Covered in wild flowers.
My brother clutched my arm and choked.

And when they lowered you into the ground
Below the apple tree,
I was the last to leave:

Tears unstoppable because that childhood was so long ago
And because you never know how much you love until it's gone.

Five Stages

It doesn't really matter what you've lost:
Whether it's the flatline on the bedside monitor,
The single hair upon the empty pillow
Or the absence of an incoming text,
You will have to learn that the book of memory
Can still be read but there is nothing more to write.

Whatever it is you've lost
It will always be the same:

Perhaps I'll wake and find it all a dream
We'll meet again in heaven
He's still in love with me.

Life is so unfair
God does not care
Why me?
I hate her for leaving me so soon
I hate myself because it must have been my fault.

O God, if I am good, can I have him back?
Dear love, I will do anything
If you give me one more chance.

Nothing matters any more.
Today I will not rise from bed.
In my heart I howl.

She is not coming back.
The sun comes up tomorrow.
The book of memory is filled with joy.
It is not a betrayal
To live
To laugh
To love again.

And in getting there
It helps to look around.
To see the light in a tree of autumn gold
And find that there is beauty when something dies.
To watch the mist lift from the lake at dawn
And know that beneath every shroud
There is a child called hope.

In 1969, the Swiss psychiatrist Elisabeth Kübler-Ross developed a model for the experience of grief, outlining five emotional stages in bereavement. Subsequently, she stressed that the stages (denial, anger, bargaining, depression, acceptance) are not a linear and predictable progression: they may occur in any order, sometimes selectively, even simultaneously. And they may not occur at all.

Moments of Exequy

Minister
Footfalls on the tarmac drive:
You came out of the darkness
On the night my father died.
For you, it was more or less
Routine and, if not easy,
Then less hard than ministry
Where you began
In the South Sudan.
For me, few words, but a presence
That assured me of his grace.

Schoolmaster
Hannibal's rock-blast vinegar fired you
To prove that Nero was a Christian emperor.
Vituperative, conspiratorial,
Were you the last lone scholar?
Only the voices of the past when you died.

Aunt
Empty house by the sea
Empty chair by the fire
The garden overgrown
The damp air clotted
with death. Her absence.

The Memory Bank

She wandered lonely as
She scratched her fingers along care-home walls
Badged with the name of Doctor Alzheimer
No one could penetrate the world under
The wisps of hair and blue-veined eggshell skull

Where a voice was whispering the Song of Songs
It was her first lover

> *Your two breasts are like two fawns*
> *Twins of a gazelle*
> *Feeding among the lilies*

And a voice was making her learn old rhymes
It was her own mother

> *A thing of beauty is a joy for ever*
> *Into my heart an air that kills*
> *And dances with the daffodils*
> *Thou'lt come no more – never never never*

And every time she heard his voice or hers
She smiled because time wound backwards
and she was who she was

Lochbroom Elegy

(IN MEMORY OF CHRISTOPHER AND TRISH MANNERS)

A rainbow lights the sky of Wester Ross
Two boys laugh as their coracle takes in water
Swallow and Amazon childhood
Unchanged through generations

Surface things do not endure
The old estate was broken up
Dry rot rose through the dark beams of Braemoor
Death and taxes: the only certainties

So they set dynamite to the big house
But you were not downcast
You did the stiff-lipped British thing
Found a little place beside the loch

Made it yours, returned each summer
Laughed through squall and midge-cloud
Walked dogs over tussock and peat
Taught names and lore to the children:

Mackenzie (Seaforth Highlanders)
Tartan of the junior pipe band
The forest of Inverlael
The peat moss on Stac Pollaidh

And let us not forget
Beinn Dearg, the mountain
Grandchildren called Ben and Jerry
In hope of ice-cream treats.

When we stopped by the road
Climbed to the cairn and looked to the west
We saw two fulmars gliding
Over the Summer Isles

As if they were your spirits
Cresting the airwaves
Young again and free
Home in your domain.

HOMAGES

The First Modern Man

Was called Francesco Petrarca

He climbed a mountain for the sole purpose
of admiring the view

He invented the love sonnet

In his imagination he traced
the steps of Odysseus

And he looked at ruins, temples and broken theatres
bringing the past back to life

No one had done these things before.

Because he reached for the distant horizon
Because he knew that love is in the yearning
Because he longed for many gods instead of one

For the return of sacred places
Spirits in river, tree and pool
Neptune rising from the waves
Diana naked in her grove
And Dionysus running riot everywhere.

Herbal

Verse being but an ornament and no cause to Poetry, since there have been many most excellent Poets that never versified.

Sir Philip Sidney

Master John Gerarde hath written of the curative properties of sundrie plantes. I say rather that their very names may soothe the spirits, for, as old Aeschylus did affirme, fine words are physick to the mind diseased.

Democritus Tertius

For each herb a bed

Meadow Grass, Red and White Dwarf in marshy ground
Great Fox-tail Grass, unprofitable

English Galingale with chaffy spikes

Norfolk Mat Weed
Bastard Camel's Hay
Small Stitchwort in form of a star,
drunk in wine with powder of acorns against pain in the side
Candy Spiderwort compact of six little leaves
of which the root tunned up in new ale
and drunk for a month together
may expel poison

Flower-de-luce is an alternative name for Iris
some are tall and great
some little
some small and low
some sweet in the root
some with no smell at all
all good in a licking medicine for shortness of breath,
the decoction also good in woman's bath
to mollify and open the matrix

Job's Tears with many knotty stalks
proceeding from a tuft of thready roots

Red Asphodil to provoke urine
Yellow Lilies for inflammation of the eyes
The Spanish Nut brings lust and lechery
Blue and White English Harebells full of juice
against the venomous bite of the field spider

A stranger: the Double White Daffodil of Constantinople

Meadow Saffron, mixed with white of eggs,
barley meal and crust of bread for a purge

The Star of Bethlehem roasted in hot embers
and applied with honey in a cataplasm
will heal old eating ulcers

And the Crown Imperial?
The vertue of this admirable plant is not yet knowne,
neither his faculties and temperature in working.

She Gave Him Eyes

She gave me eyes, she gave me ears;
And humble cares, and delicate fears;
A heart, the fountain of sweet tears;
And love, and thought, and joy.

William Wordsworth, on his sister Dorothy

You will have forgotten the day
When we two walked around the lake
Stood on the stepping stones and looked
To the soft green breast of Helm Crag
As I twined an arm around your waist

You'll want to forget that same night
When in glazed starlight we stole
Along the banked road under Silver How
Stopped to press ourselves against a drystone wall
In a lingering forbidden kiss

More likely, you remember her journals
Because what you really wanted
Was to be a sister not a lover
A sister, though, who knew she was much more
The lakeland soulmate than the wife

Did I dream that I gave you her book
Hardbound, illustrated and marked
With tender words to make those few days last?
Hoping you would forever hold our whispers,
The sights and feelings we echoed when

We lifted things of beauty from every page
Bound our two spirits through the sister's eyes:

Green paths down the hillside forming channels for streams
Withered leaves coloured with autumn yellow
Crowfoot and wild strawberries
Sheltering under hollies in fine mild rain
The sweet view up to Rydal Head
The waves around the island in the lake
Like a dance of spirits rising from the water
Reflecting purple-blue and grey

A raven high above – the dome of the sky
Echoing its call and the mountains
Giving back the sound

You with your golden hair and shining eyes
Giving me back those mountains
Giving me back my youth, my joys

A Broken Sonnet for John Clare

I loved the village ways
I loved the woods at dusk
I loved my children's laugh
I loved the threaded nest
But now
I cannot see my way
I feel a wreck within
I long for summer days
I look into the dark
But still
I joy in home and friends
I thank each tree and bush
My soul is with the nightingale
Whose freedom sings beyond asylum wall

The Thought-Crow

We called him Ted
The crow that pecked our lawn
Furious dint digger,
Guardian angel, soul in flight,
Sinister watcher.

He arrived with the shepherd's hut,
Hopped, stabbed and cawed
For month upon month

Until the day the work was done.
Early the next morning
Dew still falling and mist still lifting

I went to clear the pile of books
And a dead crow was lying on the lawn
Its head nowhere to be seen.

The Elocutionary Disappearance
of Stéphane Mallarmé

L'oeuvre pure implique la disparition élocutoire du poëte, qui cède l'initiative aux mots...

Mallarmé, *Crise de vers*

(i) *Sea Breeze*
Flesh sad, all the books read,
Escape, birds intoxicated
      on waves and skies unknown,
Nothing to hold back the heart
      trembling for the sea,
Not the old garden reflected in the eye,
Nor at night the circle of lamplight
      on the blank paper and its accusing white,
Not the lover, the baby, the milky breast.
Vanish, embark for exotic parts,
Raise anchor.

Boredom, dashed hopes,
The *adieu* of handkerchiefs.
Perhaps the raised sail, the fertile islands:
Siren song of the heart.

63

(ii) *Letter to Henri Cazalis*
The only end of the world
is a beautiful book

The only thing that really exists
is beauty

The only perfect expression
of the only thing that really exists
is poetry

Everything else is a lie

Except
in the life of the body: love
in the life of the mind: friendship

His Master's Voice
(New Place, April 1616)

Shakespeare, Drayton, and Ben Jonson had a merry meeting and it seems drank too hard, for Shakespeare died of a fever there contracted.

John Ward, Vicar of Holy Trinity Church,
Stratford-upon-Avon

Old Drayton is a lightweight, is he not?
These North Warwick men cannot stay the course.
He's mounted and off away to Polesworth.

Another measure, Ben?
And then to one more of our wit-combats.
In my mind's eye I see 'twill be the last.
They call you the old Spanish galleon:
Well-freighted but slow. And me the English
Man-of-war: lesser in bulk, but light in sail,
To turn with every tide, tack about and
Take advantage of all winds, by quickness
Of rapier wit and sheer invention.
Remember when you wrote your epitaph:
'Here lies Ben Jonson that was once one...'
And gave it me to finish, so I wrote,
'Who while he lived was a slow thing
And now being dead is no thing.'

Stay a moment, Ben. Wait for me to finish.
You've vented word mountains often enough.
You would never stoop to seek advice.
But if you did, I'd say two things, my friend.
Yes, you must *live*, hilt to point. To fill the book
And volume of the brain – that is a hunger shared.
And let the heat flow through the blood – you feared
Nor rage nor love. Your little verse for your dead boy,
Calling him your best piece of poetry:
That was brave. I could ne'er have faced my poor
Hamnet's ghost so nearly.

                                        But you have too
Much of society. Those nights at the Mermaid,
You and Beaumont and the rest. Those filled cups,
The mornings when you wake so green and pale.
And the time you waste with patrons, the Lord
Of Penshurst, Countess Lucy and the court.
You forget the other demand of art:
Solitary labour, silence, cunning.
'Tis true, what Beeston the player says:
I was not a company keeper,
Lived apart in Shoreditch, wouldn't be debauched,
And if invited on the town would plead ill health.
So here's my counsel: seldom seen is wished for seen.

And here's the second thing, the trick of art.
'Tis all in the voice. That is where you fall:
Every line you write is stamped with voice of Ben,
Whatever the humour of the player.
My stage was an island of many voices.
Remember my Jaques? Yes, his melancholy
Was some mockery of your 'humours' –
But his seven ages, remember that?
Each age was a *voice*: the infant mewling,
The schoolboy whining, lover sighing,
The soldier swearing, justice preaching,
Old man piping, whistling, trebling.
And only at the last, oblivion,
The rest that is silence.

So play the different voices, some dozen,
Twenty, thirty in a show. That's all I ever did.
Learn to lose your shape. Dislimn like a cloud,
Dissolve into your characters.
Give the actors room. Step into the wings.
You need a little of my vanishing.

Sir, I am vexed.
Bear with my weakness, my old brain is troubled:
Be not disturbed with my infirmity.
If you be pleased, retire into my cell
And there repose. A turn or two I'll walk
To still my beating mind.

CARPE DIEM

Advice to a Young Man

You can always trust a seaman:
Don't sail too close to the wind,
Don't tack too close to the shore,
Make the golden mean your grail.
The unhappiest people of all
Are the very rich and the very poor.
I heartily recommend that you don't
Aspire to be a forest pine:
The taller they grow the harder they fall,
The bigger the mountain the louder the storm.
Best to rein in both hope and fear:
Rain today doesn't mean rain tomorrow.
All you need is a little courage
When things are going badly.
And when they're going well?
Just don't be too cocky:
That's the moment to haul in your canvas.

After Horace, Odes, *II. x*

Ode

You really should not ask the question.
You're not allowed to know
When the end is coming
To me, to you.

Don't ask a fortune-teller.
You'll do much better, girl,
To treat the future like the past:
Forget it.

Whether you've many winters still to come,
Or whether your last will be this bitter one
That whips the cliff-eroding sea,
Be wise: have a drink and accept

That life is short, so hope should not be long.
In the few moments you've been listening to me,
Envious time has slid away.
Seize the day; don't trust tomorrow.

After Horace, Odes, *I. xi*

AFTERWORD

Like many people, I began writing poetry as a teenager – usually when in love, or repining with unrequited love, or trying to restore a broken heart. But also when seeing things with fresh, child-like eyes – the flight of a bird, sunlight on Tuscan stone, the rustle in the nook of a wood. Discovering the great poets made me want to be a poet myself, though the more I read of them, the more I came to realise that my true vocation was to do what I could to assist in keeping their work alive. So over the years, and as I became a teacher of literature and a writer of various kinds of literary prose, the poetry fell away. Its recent return has rather surprised me, but there is a proximate cause.

Hungry for poetry in difficult circumstances, such as the long wait in a paediatric intensive care unit, and inspired by the example of *Poems on the Underground*, those little oases of calm in the turbulence of London life, my wife, the biographer Paula Byrne, and I established ReLit, a small charitable foundation devoted to a version of the ancient art of 'bibliotherapy': the idea that slow, meditative reading may be a remedy for stress. We began by publishing the anthology *Stressed Unstressed: Classic Poems to Ease the Mind*, by delivering a 'massive open online course' on the subject of *Literature and Mental Health: Reading for Wellbeing*, and by commissioning a randomised controlled trial on the relative efficacy of a mindfulness exercise and the reading of poetry. Many people to whom we spoke about our work, and many more who took the online course, remarked that writing poetry as well as reading it may also have a therapeutic value, and so I began testing that proposition on myself by composing some new poems and resurrecting (which meant revising) some older ones. And when I shared a few of them, people kindly and gently said, 'Why not publish them, perhaps in aid of the Foundation?' So that is what I have done, using the old model of publication by subscription, which was common in the eighteenth century and was once attempted by my beloved John Clare – unsuccessfully, alas, despite the book being his very best, *A Midsummer Cushion*. Subscription was also the original publication plan for another of my favourite volumes of poetry, A. E. Housman's *A Shropshire Lad*. So I am grateful to Unbound for reviving this method of joining writers to readers and deeply indebted to all the supporters of this book.

I find poetry in rhythm, in images, and in the slowness afforded by word-compression, line-endings and the ample white spaces around the text. I offer only infrequent rhymes and little, I hope, by way of opacity. These poems and free translations are, accordingly, meant neither for those who abhor free verse nor for lovers of the avant-garde. If some of the images, emotions and thoughts bring a few moments of easeful stopping, the odd smile in recognition of a feeling shared, or the occasional leap of the heart, the collection will have offered its small measure of mental nutrition.

ABOUT THE AUTHOR

Jonathan Bate, Provost of Worcester College, Oxford, is well known as a biographer, critic, broadcaster and scholar. His creative works include a novel, *The Cure for Love*, and a one-man play for Simon Callow, *Being Shakespeare*, which toured nationally and played at the Edinburgh Festival Fringe prior to three West End runs and a transfer to New York and Chicago. He was consultant curator for *Staging the World*, the British Museum's major Shakespeare exhibition for the London 2012 Cultural Olympiad.

Jonathan Bate's many publications include *The Genius of Shake-speare*, described by Sir Peter Hall as 'the best modern book on Shakespeare'; a biography of the poet John Clare that won Britain's two oldest literary awards, the Hawthornden Prize and the James Tait Black Prize; and, most recently, a biography of Ted Hughes that was runner-up for the Samuel Johnson Prize and, in the USA, winner of the Biographers International Organization Award for the best Arts and Literature biography of 2015. He is married to the writer Paula Byrne, and they have three children.

ABOUT THE ILLUSTRATOR

Emma Bridgewater is Britain's best-known and most-loved ceramic manufacturer. Her memoir *Toast and Marmalade: Stories from the Kitchen Dresser* tells the story of her life and work. She has illustrated *The Shepherd's Hut* using the spongeware technique of her pottery.

ACKNOWLEDGEMENTS

With thanks to the only begetters, who (mostly) know who they are.

And to my teachers and superiors in the art: Peter Jay, Glen Cavaliero, Robert Fitzgerald. Also to Ian Huish for support and Jack Lankester and Sally Bayley for advice on inclusions and exclusions.

To everyone in the team at Unbound. And *especially* to Emma Bridgewater for her illustrations.

A handful of these poems have been previously published. Thanks to *Wicked Ant*, *The Harvard Advocate*, the *Guardian* and the anthology published by William Collins, *Stressed Unstressed*. The dramatic monologue imagining Shakespeare's last meeting with Ben Jonson is an (unperformed) offshoot from my one-man play for Simon Callow, which began life as *The Man from Stratford* and became *Being Shakespeare*.

With special thanks to H. R. H. Nazrin Shah,
Sultan of Perak, Malaysia

SUPPORTERS

Unbound is a new kind of publishing house. Our books are funded directly by readers. This was a very popular idea during the late eighteenth and early nineteenth centuries. Now we have revived it for the internet age. It allows authors to write the books they really want to write and readers to support the books they would most like to see published.

The names listed below are of readers who have pledged their support and made this book happen. If you'd like to join them, visit www.unbound.com.

Verónica Allen
Min Angel
Kim Baker
Sally Bayley
Graham Blenkin
Paul Blezard
William Broyles
Felicity Bryan
Angie Burke
Paula Byrne
Jonathan Chamberlain
Sue Childs
Julian Clyne
Becky Cole
John and Heather Crease

Richard Crease
Alex Cross
Julia Croyden
Peter Davidson
Carol Davies
Philip Davis
Claire Durbin
Paul Edwards
Emilio Englade
Paul Forster
Hayden Gabriel
Nick Gammage
Tim Gee
Mick Gowar
Hillary Hammond

Margaret Harris

Tim Hipperson

Ian Huish

Mark Inch

Steven Jackson

David Jones

Sean Jones

Michele Lynn Kaminski

Peter Kettle

Dan Kieran

Patrick Kincaid

Jack Lankester

Paul Levy

Caroline Lim

Marie-Louise Avery Linklater

Tamasin Little

Evadne Lucas

Catherine Mac Mahon

Melanie Martin

John Mitchinson

Bel Mooney

Carmel Morgan

Carlo Navato

Pamela Nixon

Julia O'Brien

Barbara O'Shea

Nicky Parkinson

Mark Lindsay Parsons

Sarah Patmore

Dan Peters

Justin Pollard

Jeff Potter

Robert Pymm

Sophie Ratcliffe

Liam Riley

Lorna Robson

Elizabeth Rublack-Diamond

James Sainsbury

Matthew Salisbury and
    Jennifer Rushworth

Arijana Schrauwen

Andrew Schuman

HRH Sultan Nazrin Shah

Mike Simmonds

Joan Slecka

Karen Elizabeth Smith

Carolyn Soakell

Charmian Steven

Christina Strickland

Plum Sykes

Laura Thompson

Rebecca Thorpe

Harold Walker

Sir John Weston

Gail Whyte

Barrie and Deedee Wigmore

Kate Woodhead